IMAGES
of Sport

READING
FOOTBALL CLUB
1871-1997

The Mayor of Reading, Alderman C.F. Clark, shakes hands with Reading centre-forward Ron Blackman before the Festival of Britain match against the National Club of Luxembourg. The game, played at Elm Park on 16 May 1951, resulted in a 4–0 victory for Reading.

IMAGES
of Sport

READING
FOOTBALL CLUB
1871-1997

Compiled by
David Downs

TEMPUS

First published 1997, reprinted 2001
Copyright © David Downs, 1997

Tempus Publishing Limited
The Mill, Brimscombe Port,
Stroud, Gloucestershire, GL5 2QG

ISBN 0 7524 1061 X

Typesetting and origination by
Tempus Publishing Limited
Printed in Great Britain by
Midway Colour Print, Wiltshire

Cover picture:
The view from the Tilehurst End during a first-team game at Elm Park
in the early 1950s when attendances averaged over 15,000.

Contents

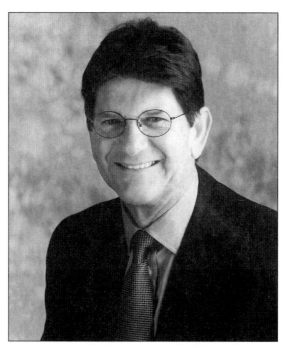

Foreword

By the Chairman of Reading Football Club, John Madejski

As we move into the most exciting period in the history of Reading Football Club, it is not only a time for looking forward but also a time for reflecting on the past and the many wonderful memories we share of the club and, in particular, of Elm Park, our home for 101 years.

This book traces the club's rich history through a fascinating series of photographs: from a nostalgic look back at the very early years to a celebration of recent events and achievements.

Every Reading supporter will find a picture which stirs a host of memories and reminds them why the club and Elm Park have meant so much to us all through the years. Those memories can now be relived again and again as we commemorate the end of our time at Elm Park with a definitive pictorial record of the story so far.

David Downs has done a remarkable job in compiling this book and highlighting many great occasions and personalities from years gone by. The result is a fitting tribute to Elm Park and the part it has played in our lives.

I feel very privileged to be able to preside over Reading Football Club at this moment in time as we close one remarkable chapter in the history of the club and move into what promises to be a new and even more remarkable era.

I am sure this book will give many people an immense amount of pleasure, both now and in the future, and I hope that in years to come it will enable us to look back on our time at Elm Park with pride, joy, and affection.

John Madejski

Introduction and Acknowledgments

The demolition of Elm Park will have the same emotional effect on many people as the loss of an elderly and much-loved relation, though maybe one who has only been visited once a fortnight, for such is the affinity that supporters of Reading FC have with the town's home of football. For more than a century it has been the venue to exchange gossip, news, opinions, and also to experience the whole range of feelings from hope and anticipation, through excitement or despair, to delight or sadness.

I shall be devastated at the disappearance of Elm Park, but I feel privileged to have the opportunity of recording the history of the club before and during its time at the ground. I almost literally cut my teeth on the boundary wall under the clock on the Tilehurst Road side in the late 1940s, and I have watched many triumphs and disasters in the following fifty years. I remember the great names of my childhood – players like Blackman, Brice, and Edelston – when Elm Park was all about packed crowds, rattles and rosettes, goalmouth scrambles, and when Reading were invincible at home. The 1950s seemed almost drab by comparison, but there was always the cultured wing-half play of Anderton and Evans, plus the acrobatics of goalkeeper Jones, to brighten gloomy Saturday afternoons. The club meandered along quite comfortably in Division Three throughout the 1960s, but the 1970s and 1980s brought the constant highs and lows of promotion and relegation before Reading eventually became established in the modern First Division. Particular highlights during that time were the 3–0 win at Port Vale to win Division Four and enable that brave little goalkeeper Steve Death to set a Football League record by remaining unbeaten for eleven consecutive matches, and the 2–0 victory at Newport County which also set a record as the team won its twelfth league match from the start of the season. Then, there was the greatest day of all – the Simod Cup success at Wembley on 27 March 1988.

As one who is besotted with Reading Football Club – I once rang the Samaritans to find out the result of an away game when the television was on the blink – I have been grateful for the kindness and co-operation of like-minded supporters and ex-players who have allowed me access to their own scrapbooks and memorabilia. I wish to record my thanks to Gary Arkell, James Ashford, Clive Baskerville of the *Reading Evening Post*, Simon Eedle, Maurice Evans, Kevin Girdler, Bryan Horsnell, Bryan McAllister, Gordon Neate, Helen Peterson, Ben Redgrove, Tim Redgrove, Alan Sedunary, Richard Shepherd, Ray Simmonds, Steven Smith of Haslams, Geoff Thompson, Douggie Webb, and Bobby Williams. I am also grateful to Marion for her infinite patience while I have been collating and writing, staff at Chalford Publishing for their advice, the many photographers to whose skill the book is a testimony, and the generations of supporters and players who have made Reading Football Club such an important part of people's lives over the past 126 years.

From Biscuits to Royals, Elm Park to the Madejski Stadium, Southern League to Division One, this is the pictorial history of Reading FC. I have been totally absorbed and fascinated in compiling it, and I hope it will have the same effect on its readers. Up the Royals!

David Downs
September 1997

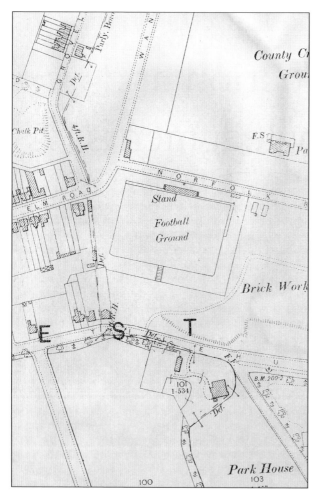

The 1898 Ordnance Survey map of the west Reading area shows how little housing then surrounded Elm Park, which had opened two years previously. The four-acre site had been leased to Reading FC by Councillor Jesse of Castle Hill House. The site had formerly been used as a gravel pit for the Jesse Estate building works, hence its proximity to the brickworks.

One
Gentlemen and Players
(1871–1920)

The first Reading Football Club team, which played a series of friendly matches during the 1871–72 season against teams from Berkshire, Buckinghamshire, and Oxfordshire. Not a single game was lost during that first season. Among the playing members of the club were J.W. Martin, later to become mayor of Reading, and Edward Haygarth, who played for England in 1875. Mr James Sydenham (wearing ordinary attire, back row) volunteered to act as the club's first honorary secretary.

On 26 March 1892 Reading won the Berks & Bucks Senior Cup by beating Wolverton 2–0 with goals from Warburton and Hewitt. The line-up was, from left to right, back row: J. Warburton, H.V. Hewitt, H.E. Walker (secretary), T. Skurray, J. Manners; middle row: C. White, J. George, F. Deane (captain), S.D. Justins, E. Harrowell; front: J. Vennard, H. Read.

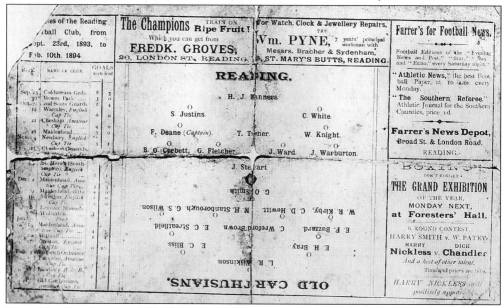

The oldest Reading Football Club programme in existence was printed for the FA Amateur Cup tie against Old Carthusians on 17 February 1894. A crowd estimated at 1,000 watched the game, played at Caversham, and saw Reading lose 4–1.

READING FOOTBALL CLUB.

SATURDAY, September 5th, 1896.

OPENING OF THE SPLENDID NEW GROUND

AT ELM PARK,

BY

C. T. MURDOCH, Esq., M.P.

AT 3.30 P.M.

READING

(SOUTHERN LEAGUE TEAM) play

A. ROSTON BOURKE'S LONDON XI

ADMISSION 6d. Ladies and Boys Half-price. ENCLOSURE 3d. extra.

THE READING TEMPERANCE PRIZE BAND will attend.

TRAMS and **BUSSES** run close to Ground.

PETTY & SONS, Ltd., READING.

After playing matches at Reading Recreation Ground, Reading Cricket Ground, Coley Park, and Caversham Cricket Ground, Reading eventually settled on Elm Park as their home base. The first match, advertised by this poster, resulted in a 7–1 win for Reading against a London XI.

The first Reading FC board of directors, 1896. From left to right, standing: J. Sharp, P. Cohen, W. Rideout; sitting: H. Childs, J. Warburton, J.R. Blandford. Mr Blandford once played for Reading reserves at Fulham in an emergency when he was 70 years of age!

The Reading team which played in Elm Park's opening fixture on 5 September 1896 was, from left to right, back row: Babes, Justins (captain), Cannon, Watts; middle row: Spiers, Bach, Wheeler; front row: Hadley, G. Reid, J. Reid, Cunningham.

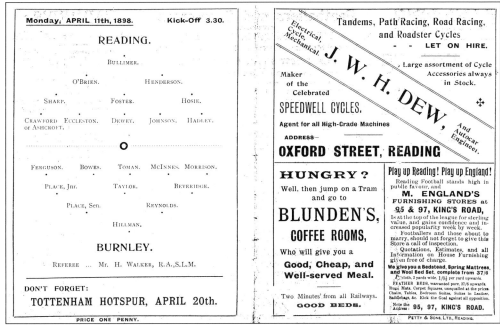

A programme from Reading's second season at Elm Park showing the teams for a fixture against Burnley on 11 April 1898. Although Reading were competing in the Southern League, they frequently played end-of-season friendly matches against Football League clubs to increase revenue.

This FA Cup tie at Elm Park in the 1903–04 season saw a 'moderate' crowd of 8,765 watch Reading draw 1–1 with Bolton Wanderers of the Football League. Goalkeeper Naisby (centre) is about to clear a Bolton attack. Reading lost the replay 3–2.

13

Herbert Smith (left), seen here playing for England against Scotland at the Crystal Palace on 1 April 1905, was one of Reading's greatest players. He joined the club in 1902 and captained the Southern League team. He won 4 full international caps for England and 17 amateur caps. He played at full-back and was known as 'a total abstainer'.

Fred Bartholemew joined Reading FC as an amateur on Good Friday, 1904, having previously played for the Reading Biscuit Factory team. He turned professional three years later, and eventually retired as a player in 1923. During the First World War he joined the Footballers' Battalion and saw active service, reaching the rank of CQMS (company quarter-master sergeant). At the end of his playing career he became the Elm Park groundsman and continued in that role until the 1950s enjoying the nickname of 'Old Bart'.

A view of Elm Park just after the turn of the century with Reading about to kick off in a Southern League match. By now Reading were fielding a team of mainly professional players, and the ground had been upgraded to cater for crowds approaching 10,000.

READING FOOTBALL TEAM, 1904-5.

H. Matthews (*Sec.*)   Naisby.   Riley.   Bannister.   Raisbeck.   F. Paley (*Trainer*).   H. Smith (*Capt.*)
Henderson.   McIntyre.   Higginson.   Cummings.   Harris.   Crombie.
Bainbridge.   Long.   Corrin.

The Reading team of 1904–05 had a successful season in the Southern League First Division, finishing as runners-up to the champions, Bristol Rovers. Reading were also joint winners of the Southern Charity Cup, drawing 0–0 with Tottenham Hotspur in the final.

READING FOOTBALL CLUB, LIMITED, 1908-9.

G. Hancock.   W. Rogers.   A. Crump.   A. Newbigging.   F. Wilkes.   J. Boden.
F. Burch.   A. Leonard.   G. Willis.   F. G. Wheatcroft.   J. Huggins.   C. Mainds.

Photo by Everard Cuzner,   Vandyck Studio, Reading

There had been a complete change of personnel from the 1904–05 line-up by the time this picture of the 1908–09 team was taken.

Action from a Southern League fixture between Reading and Norwich City at Elm Park on Saturday, 21 November 1908, with Reading about to take a corner kick at the Tilehurst end of the ground. Reading finished eighth in the First Division of the Southern League that season.

Reading had been relegated from Division One of the Southern League in 1910, but regained their place by winning Division Two in the 1910–11 season. The crowd gathered to watch the presentation of the trophy after the final game of the season, a 5–0 home win over Chesham Town.

The Reading team and supporters line up in preparation for the 1911–12 season, proudly displaying the Southern League Division Two trophy. In the centre of the front row is Alan Foster, who was killed in action in the First World War.

One of Reading's best performances as a Southern League club was to defeat Aston Villa of the Football League's First Division in an FA Cup replay. Reading won 1–0 at Elm Park in 1912, Foster scoring the goal. Goalkeeper Caldwell is pictured jumping to punch the ball away while under considerable pressure in the Reading goalmouth.

After beating Aston Villa, Reading were drawn at home to Manchester United in the third round; a new attendance record was set for Elm Park with a crowd of 24,069 producing gate receipts of £1,350. Reading, in stripes, were outplayed for most of the game, but forced a 1–1 draw before losing the replay at Old Trafford.

This programme contained the teams for a Southern League match between Reading and Millwall at Elm Park on 12 September 1914. Also in the programme were advertisements for Jackson's Café and the Temperance Hotel in West Street, and the George Hotel in Broad Street. Syd Crawford, Reading's goalkeeper in the match, was transferred to Millwall in 1922 for a fee of £50.

A variety of headgear was sported by spectators at the Bournemouth versus Reading match played at Bournemouth on 4 April 1914. A nonchalant pose is adopted by the gentleman in the centre of the front row, who looks as though he has arrived at the game either by aeroplane or motor-cycle!

The Reading FC squad for the 1914–15 season, at the end of which the club finished as runners-up in Division One of the Southern League. From left to right, back row (players only): Bartholemew, Chorley, Seed, Crawford, Thomson, Willis, Ralphs; middle row: Rowlands, Stevens, Bailey, Smith, Foster, Green, Comrie; front row: Campbell, Getgood, Lofthouse.

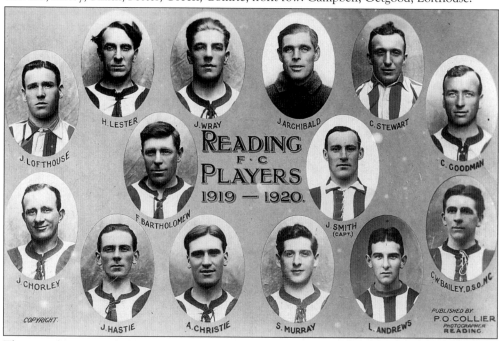

This was the group of players who represented Reading during the 1919–20 season, the club's last in the Southern League. At the end of the season the Southern League First Division clubs, Reading among them, applied to join the Football League. They were all accepted as associate members in a newly-formed Division Three. Reading's final Southern League match was a 2–0 away win against Luton Town on 1 May 1920.

Two

The Glory Days (1920–1931)

The Reading team at the start of the 1925–26 season, in which Reading became champions of Division Three (South). From left to right, standing: A.E. Clifford (director), Wilson, Inglis, Messer, Duckworth, McConnell, Evans, J. Jackson (trainer); sitting: Smith, Braithwaite, Davey, Tinsley, Robson.

Reading F.C. 1920-1921.

yrs faithfully.
"Joe" Bailey.

Collier
Photo
Reading

The team which represented Reading FC at the beginning of the 1920–21 season, their first in the Football League. From left to right, back row: H. Marshall (secretary/manager), Christie, Mavin, Smith, Crawford, Horler, Getgood, F. Wilkes (trainer); sitting: Spence, Bailey, Yarnell, Andrews, Carr. Reading finished twentieth out of twenty-two teams in Division Three. Bailey was the leading scorer with seventeen goals.

W.G. ('Joe') Bailey was a Reading hero both on and off the field. He played for the club in the Southern League and the Football League, and scored Reading's first Football League goal in a 1–0 away win against Newport County on 28 August 1920. He also represented Berkshire at cricket and Oxfordshire at hockey. During the First World War he reached the rank of captain in the Middlesex Regiment and was decorated four times for bravery, winning the Distinguished Service Order and Military Cross with two bars.

READING *V.* CHELSEA.

The programme for the FA Cup replay between Reading and Chelsea at Stamford Bridge on 12 January 1921 included a cartoon describing the 0–0 draw between the teams in the previous match. It made some scathing references to the Elm Park ground, but paid tribute to Reading goalkeeper Syd Crawford, whose last-minute penalty save had ensured the replay. The replay was also drawn, 2–2, but Reading were beaten in the third match 3–1.

Reading captain Len Grant is presented with the trophy after Reading had beaten Brighton & Hove Albion 2–1 at Elm Park for the Royal Berkshire Hospital Charity Cup at the end of the 1923–24 season. The fixture began in 1921 to raise funds for the hospital, and after the first match against Southampton ended in a brawl, Brighton became the annual opponents until 1928, when the fixture was discontinued. The magnificent cup cost its donor, Mr R.J. Tyrell, £150, and Messrs McIlroys presented gold medals each year to the winning team, and silver-plated tankards to the runners-up.

A goalmouth mêlée during the Reading versus Bristol Rovers league match, played at Elm Park on 5 April 1926, with Braithwaite (left) and Richardson challenging the Rovers defenders for the ball. Reading won the game 3–0 to maintain their push for promotion to Division Two.

Reading became champions of Division Three (South) by defeating Brentford 7–1 at Elm Park on the last day of the 1925–26 season. *Above*: centre-forward Frank Richardson scores the first of the Reading goals. *Below*: a section of the large crowd which assembled in front of the grandstand to celebrate at the end of the match.

Caricatures drawn for the local paper of the Reading team which began the 1926–27 season. It was to be a momentous year for the club, in which it would reach the FA Cup semi-final, and also fourteenth position in Division Two, the club's highest placing thus far in its history.

Reading's first win after promotion to Division Two came with a 4–0 victory against Nottingham Forest on 4 September 1926. Robson scored Reading's second goal (*above*), while Richardson obtained the third (*below*). A crowd of 17,428, paying a total of £925, watched the game.

Elm Park's record attendance of 33,042 was set at the FA Cup fifth-round tie against Brentford on 19 February 1927. A goal by Frank Richardson as the Brentford goalkeeper misjudged his shot (above) gave Reading a 1–0 victory.

More action from the FA Cup tie between Reading and Brentford as Braithwaite (second from left) watches a Reading attack end with Richardson (right) following a shot past the post. The tightly-packed crowd in Elm Park's highest attendance can clearly be seen in the background.

A composite picture of the Reading team which played Cardiff City in the FA Cup semi-final in the 1926–27 season, taken from a programme published by the Reading Newspaper Company. The players, in formation, are from the top, left to right: Duckworth (goalkeeper), Eggo and McConnell (full-backs), Inglis, Messer, and Evans (half-backs), McDonald, Braithwaite, Johnstone, Richardson, and Robson (forwards). McConnell was an Irish international and Evans had played for Wales.

The FA Cup semi-final against Cardiff City at Wolverhampton Wanderers' Molineux ground on 26 March 1927 proved to be a great disappointment for Reading and their supporters as they were beaten 3–0. *Above*: the captains, Eggo (Reading) and Keenor (Cardiff City), shake hands before the kick-off. *Below*: a Reading attack ends with McDonald shooting just wide.

Two of the Cardiff City goals, as Ferguson (*above*) shoots past Duckworth, and (*below*) a header from Wake eludes McConnell and Duckworth. This was Reading's first and, so far, only appearance in this stage of the competition.

It was back to league action after the disappointment of the semi-final, and Reading beat Port Vale 2–0 at Elm Park to finish fourteenth in the Second Division. Johnstone was foiled by the visiting goalkeeper on this occasion, as were the supporting players, Richardson and Robson.

The Reading FC players seen in a more relaxed mood after the exertions of the 1926–27 season, enjoying a garden party which enabled them to show their prowess at other sports.

A collection of mementos featuring goalkeeper Joe Duckworth, who made over two hundred appearances for Reading between 1924 and 1930. His Division Three (South) championship medal was found in a car-boot sale in Manchester in 1991, 65 years after he had won it.

Frank Richardson played far fewer games for the club, but his 47 goals in just 91 league matches, including this diving header against Preston North End, contributed greatly to Reading's glory days in the late 1920s. Richardson returned to Reading after the Second World War to help with the running of the club's youth and minor teams.

On 28 January 1928 Reading entertained Leicester City in the fourth round of the FA Cup. A crowd of more than 28,000 saw the visitors win by a single goal to nil. The Norfolk Road grandstand was now complete but the only other covered accommodation in the ground was at the back of the Tilehurst Road terracing.

READING F.C. MANAGEMENT CRITICISED

Lively Discussions Between Shareholders and Directors.

SUPPORTERS' CLUB TO BE FORMED ?

The extraordinary meeting of the Reading Football Club, which was held at Olympia on Monday evening, was in some ways disappointing, for although more than two hours were spent in discussing matters concerning the club, not one concrete resolution or proposal likely to improve the position of the team in the Second League was put to the shareholders. The meeting was called in response to a petition of the shareholders, and it gave many a chance to express their views and in some cases to criticise the directors, manager, other officials and the players.

The most encouraging feature of the meeting was provided by Canon F. J. C. Gillmor, who said the directors had that day received a letter which suggested that there was a probability of a supporters' club being formed. The coffers of the club are not too well lined, and in the present crucial moment the directors will doubtless welcome the inauguration of any organisation which will help them in their endeavours to improve the team in order that they may escape relegation.

CLUB'S FINANCIAL STRESS.

The first football supporters' club was formed following an extraordinary general meeting of Reading FC called because of its poor playing and financial position. The inaugural meeting of the Supporters' Club was held on 7 December 1930, and Mr H. Sirett, editor of the *Football Chronicle*, was elected chairman. Membership cost one shilling per year. The club was disbanded in the early 1950s but reformed in 1954, and has continued to act as a link between fans and directors.

Left: although just 5ft 9in tall Hugh Davey was one of our most prolific forwards, scoring 46 goals in 62 league games between 1924 and 1928. He was the top scorer in the Third Division (South) championship season, with 23 goals in just 24 games. He also gained five Irish international caps while with Reading, scoring against England in 1925. *Right*: Arthur Bacon, who holds the record for the highest number of goals scored in a game by a Reading player. He netted six times in the 7–3 victory over Stoke City at Elm Park on Good Friday, 1931. His total of 29 goals during the 1930–31 season, however, was not sufficient to save the club from relegation to Division Three (South).

A popular method of transport to Elm Park during the 1920s and 1930s was the tram service which operated from Broad Street. Those who preferred to walk or could not afford the tram fare could march behind the band which played all the way from the centre of town to Norfolk Road.

Left: despite losing their place in Division Two, Reading enjoyed several FA Cup triumphs against teams from higher divisions. A 1–0 win over Sheffield Wednesday was marked by the issue of this memorial card. *Right*: Alf Messer, an outstanding centre-half, who was tipped for an England cap on several occasions. He played 272 league matches for Reading between 1923 and 1930 and his transfer to Tottenham Hotspur was the final blow to Reading's hopes of avoiding relegation in 1931.

Three

Goals, Guests and Gas Masks (1931–1948)

The Reading team and officials at the start of the 1935–36 season, at the end of which Reading finished third in Division Three (South). From left to right, back row: McGough, Butler, Robson, Mapson, Whittaker, Wildman, Hayhurst, Darvill, Gregory; middle row: Penny (trainer), Ludley (director), Wadkson (director), Duguid (director), Boyle, Dollery, Fielding, Wright, Bartholemew (groundsman), Clifford (director), Clancy (trainer), Bray (secretary), Butler (manager); front row: Fitzgerald, Briggs, McMahon, Liddle, Townsend, Johnson, Telling, Tait, Paterson, Keetley, Done.

Joe McGough (*left*) and (*below*) scoring in a 3–1 home win over Northampton Town on 10 April 1937, was a mainstay in the Reading attack between 1932 and 1938. Playing at inside-forward he made 142 league appearances and scored 50 goals. He weighed just over nine stone when he joined the club, and was told by the manager to drink a bottle of Guinness every evening to build up his strength! He was transferred from Reading to Chester for £500, and in his later years always made a point of watching games between the two teams.

CORINTH NOT GOOD ENOUGH

Reading met the famous amateur club, the Corinthians, in the first round of the FA Cup at Elm Park on 30 November 1935. The amateurs scored first and in the words of Reading captain George Johnson: 'For twenty minutes they had us running round with our tongues hanging out.' Reading's superior fitness eventually told, though, and they won 8–3 with goals from Liddle (3), Tait (2), Fielding (2) and McGough. A crowd of 15,998 watched the game and gate receipts were £1,005. The result still stands as Reading's highest score in the FA Cup.

READING'S GREAT CHALLENGE

VIEWS ON THE TIE

By FRANK THOROGOOD

Reading 0   The Arsenal 1

AS Cumberworth and I passed with scrip and staff into the booking-hall at Paddington station on Saturday, one of the porters who lined up to salute our pilgrimage said to his mate : " I'll bet you what you like old Jimmy Thomas is going down to Reading " ; and sure enough the Government of the day was represented in this new deal of the Arsenal. It is true Derby County lie in their Cup-tie graves, but Mr. Thomas, with a Soccer foot in both camps still hopes to see the League champions reach the Final.

A BATCH OF INTERVIEWS

When the battle ended at Elm Park and the Arsenal had won as the result of a great goal by Bastin we not only got the views of the "Cabinet," but also of others concerned in the Cup tie. Here they are :

Mr. J. H. Thomas.—" A good, hard game, but I should have preferred a draw—a much better result on the play."

Sir Frederick Wall (now an Arsenal director). — " We just scrambled home "—and this in a whisper of relief.

Sir Samuel Hill-Wood (chairman of Arsenal).—"A typical Cup tie between First and Third League clubs."

Mr. Arthur Armitage (chairman of Reading). — " We ought not to have gone down on the play, but one of us had to lose. Good luck to the Arsenal."

Mr. Joe Smith (Reading manager).— " We were very unfortunate. Good luck to the Arsenal. I had a wire from Bolton before the match, and it read: 'Good luck to Reading. If you were playing I should have backed 'em.' Do you know, I'm 45 years old, but that telegram made me blush."

Mr. Herbert Smith (old international and former Reading captain). —" The Arsenal were very lucky, but don't put in your paper all I'm going to say to you about the good old days." The Gracie Fields of Reading (who sat behind us in the Press Box).—" Eh lad, that Bastin is a loovely player, but the Arsenal never won on their merits."

For myself I liked best the feminine view, because it was all so frankly true. In a sentence Reading richly deserved to draw. Bastin was undeniably a " loovely player," and the greatest forward afield ; but his side never rose to the majesty of First League rank—indeed, after the winning goal 20 minutes from the end Moss and his colleagues had to fight like Bulls of Bashan.

The heads of the Arsenal at that critical stage worked like mechanical piston-rods, and the best of them all belonged to the magic body of Roberts. I saw this remarkable player keep Luton out of their Cup-tie kingdom last season, and here at Reading he was the same indomitable figure, " the Red Earl of the Arsenal."

As Caesar himself might have said : " Let me have men about me who are red-headed and I will win all my battles."

Next to Roberts in defence give me Hayhurst, the Reading centre-half, who, with Gregory, Robson, Johnson and Wright, kept the Arsenal well under control, even though the home side had to contend against half a gale of wind during the opening half.

A SPOILING WIND

If it was not a good game, the wind must be regarded as chief sinner, for it did much to bring Soccer talent down to a common level. The ball was blown about the skies like the rooks in the poem.

The Arsenal forwards, never great as a combination, certainly played better against the wind. Drake, however, was not allowed, either as intrepid barger or cunning schemer, to work his will, and neither Beasley nor Birkett had the fire of Joe Hulme, who watched the game from the ring. James was spasmodic, and Bastin ever remained the star. Hapgood, injured near the end, did not reproduce his England form, and Male on the day was the better back.

BARLEY AS THE ROVER

In the Reading attack Butler and McGough were easily the most effective schemers. Though Tait for the most part was in the grip of Roberts, Barley always made an industrious, not to say vigorous, rover. Fielding, however, could not rise to the occasion.

The goal which Bastin scored at long range originated from a corner, which Wright might, perhaps, have prevented. As at Leicester, so at Reading, the Arsenal had a narrow squeak in a tie where Moss had more to do in goal than Whittaker.

Reading: Whittaker; Gregory, Robson, Johnson, Hayhurst, Wright; Butler, McGough, Tait, Barley, Fielding.

Arsenal: Moss; Male, Hapgood; Crayston, Roberts, Copping; Birkett, Bastin, Drake, James, Beasley.

Another epic FA Cup tie took place at Elm Park on 16 February 1935, when Reading lost 1–0 to the famous Arsenal team. A contemporary press report tells how close Reading came to forcing a draw.

The two captains, George Johnson of Reading (stripes) and Alex James, toss for ends watched by the referee. This was the last occasion on which Reading reached the fifth round of the FA Cup. A crowd of 30,621 paid £3,109 to watch the match.

Action from the tie as Butler and Tait of Reading challenge Moss in the Arsenal goal. Hapgood and Roberts stand by to protect their keeper.

41

Tommy Tait (stripes) scores Reading's second goal in a 2–0 victory against local rivals Aldershot at the Recreation Ground in February 1937. Reading had signed him for £1,000 from Bournemouth in 1934, with £200 of the fee being provided by the Supporters' Club. Tait, whose bustling style of centre-forward play made him popular with the fans, stayed until 1938, scoring 77 goals in 145 league matches.

THE CHORUS

The words of the chorus are:—

LET US ALL SHOUT HOORAY
TO ALL WHO PLAY TO-DAY,
LET'S BE BRIGHT AND GAY
THAT'S THE ONLY WAY,
GIVE OUR LADS A CHEER
TO HELP THEM WIN THE GAME,
WHEN THEY WIN, SHOULD THEY LOSE,
CHEER THEM JUST THE SAME.
THEY ARE THE HOPE OF ALL
THE READING FANS TO-DAY,
HELP THEM ON THEIR WAY,
MAKE THEM BRIGHT AND GAY,
LET US ALL GIVE
THREE CHEERS TO READING
AND SHOUT HIP, HIP, HOORAY !

Jack Morgan, the musical director at the Palace Theatre, Reading, composed a song to be sung by Reading supporters at home matches. It was used for the first time at Elm Park on 8 February 1936 and proved to be a success, as Reading beat Notts County 3–1 that afternoon.

Reading won the Third Division (South) Cup in the 1937–38 season by beating Bristol City 6–2 on aggregate after home and away games. Mr R.J. Kilbey, vice-chairman of Watford FC, presented the cup to Fullwood, Reading's skipper. The trophy was never competed for subsequently, and remains on display in the boardroom at Elm Park.

Pre-season training for the Reading players during the summer of 1938 included plenty of stretching exercises. This was to be the last full Football League season before the outbreak of the Second World War, and Reading finished in a respectable fifth place in Division Three (South). MacPhee was the leading scorer with 25 goals from 42 games.

43

-and a bon voyage to the new Reading F.C. directorate

The Reading FC board of directors elected at the beginning of the 1938–39 season, drawn by cartoonist Fred May. Their appearance in naval uniform was an unhappy reminder of the approach of war.

Although the Second World War had begun in September 1939, football continued at Elm Park with a series of friendly matches. Freddie Smallwood headed Reading's only goal in a 3–1 defeat by Arsenal past Bernard Joy and George Marks, with MacPhee appearing to push the visiting goalkeeper.

Reading's greatest success in wartime football, once league and cup competitions had been organised, was to beat Brentford 3–2 in the London War Cup final played at Stamford Bridge in June 1941. Pictured with the trophy are, from left to right: Joe Edelston (manager), Maurice Edelston, Jack Oxberry (trainer), Jimmy Fullwood, Tony MacPhee, Bill Layton, and Joe McPhie, a guest player from Falkirk. The players each received a 7/6 savings certificate as a win bonus.

The programme for Reading's game at Chelsea in 1943 showed the inclusion of a number of guest players such as Mercer (Everton) and Mapson (Sunderland), together with Reading players who were on leave or in reserved occupations. Spectators were advised to carry gas-masks to games and to listen out for air-raid warnings.

CHELSEA FOOTBALL CLUB

Official Programme

SATURDAY APRIL 10th 1943   PRICE ONE PENNY

CHELSEA v. READING

FOOTBALL LEAGUE SOUTH
Cup Competition   Kick-off 3.15 p.m.

CHELSEA (Blue)

WOODLEY
Goal

SMITH   HAPGOOD
Right Back (2)   Left Back (3)

FIDDES   GREENWOOD   COLLETT
Right Half (4) Centre Half (5) Left Half (6)

SPENCE   McKENNAN   MATHIE   FOSS   MILLS
Outside Right (7) Inside Right (8) Centre (9) Inside Left (10) Outside Left (11)

Referee—Mr. A. T. FORD (London)   ○   Linesmen   Mr. T. LEWIS   Red and White Flag
                                                     Mr. T. W. McCARTHY   Blue and White Flag

WILLIAMS   PATERSON   McPHEE   EDELSTON   CHITTY
Outside Left (11) Inside Left (10) Centre (9) Inside Right (8) Outside Right (7)

COLLIER   RATCLIFFE   MERCER
Left Half (6)   CentreHalf (5)   Right Half (4)

JONES   COLDBERG
Left Back (3)   Right Back (2)

MAPSON
Goal

READING (Blue and White)

THIS SEASON'S GOAL SCORERS			
McKENNAN	13	TENNANT	1
FOSS	11	AIRLIE	1
BRYANT	10	HARDWICK	1
SPENCE	8	KURZ	1
PAYNE	5	MATHIE	1
MILLS	4	SOO	1
LIDDELL	2	DEVERALL	1
BIDEWELL	1	Total	61

Future Matches

April 24 Football League South
Cup Semi-Final

April 26 Inter-Allied Services
Cup-Final

May 15 North v. South
Cup Winners

AIR RAID WARNING—In the event of an Air Raid Warning the Ground exits will be opened, so that those who wish to leave can do so. Play will proceed unless the "Spotter" reports enemy activity in the vicinity.

Francisto, London

ELM PARK

SATURDAY, APRIL 8th, 1944.

BRITISH UNITED SERVICES

v.

ALLIED UNITED SERVICES

KICK-OFF 3.0

Right Wing   *Left Wing*

BRITISH UNITED SERVICES

Sergt. W. G. Marks
(R.A.F.)

2—**Lt. J. W. Firth**   3—**Sergt. H. S. Robbins**
(Army)   (Army)

4—**P.O. T. McKillope**   5—**P.O. W. Corbett**   6—**Corp. R. Burgess**
(R. Navy)   (R. Navy)   (R.A.F.)

7—**Capt. T. P. Collins** 8—**O/Tel. T. W. Bowie** 9—**F/O E. J. Drake** 10 **C.S.M.I. M. Edelston**
(Army)   (R. Navy)   (R.A.F.)   (Army)

11 **Marine H. Cumner**
(R. Marines)

11—**L/Cpl. Czubaszek**
(Poland)

10—**C.F.T.M.N. Debusser** 9—**C.F.T.M.N. Sveinson** 8—**C.F.T.M.N. Effern** 7—**Cadet/O. Szyjka**
(Belgium)   (Norway)   (Netherlands)   (Poland)

6—**Cadet/O. Stanczyk**   5—**Sgt. Billiet**   4—**Pte. Rojahn**
(Poland)   (Belgium)   (Norway)

3—**Pte. Dujisik**   2—**Pte. Grumelon**
(Czech)   (France)

Pte. Brinkman
(Netherlands)

ALLIED UNITED SERVICES

Left Wing   *Right Wing*

Referee—Mr. C. KEARSE.
Linesmen—Messrs. L. BRUNSDON and J. DARE.

Official Team Sheet—ONE PENNY.

A number of inter-services matches were played at Elm Park during the war years. It was an ideal location for these games because it was safer than London yet near to Aldershot where many professional footballers were stationed as PT instructors. In this fixture the British team included Reading's Maurice Edelston, as well as George Marks and Ted Drake, later to join to club as goalkeeper and manager, respectively.

Reading's record victory came soon after the resumption of peacetime football. On 4 September 1946 the team beat Crystal Palace 10–2 in a Division Three (South) match at Elm Park. Maurice Edelston (hoops) scores one of his three goals in that match.

The Reading team, wearing their change strip of white shirts and blue shorts for an FA Cup match away to West Bromwich Albion in January 1948. From left to right, back row: McKenna (reserve), Goldberg, O'Sullivan, Drake (manager), Gulliver, Oxberry (trainer); middle row: Fisher, Edelston, MacPhee, Lee (chairman), Taylor, Deverall, Ratcliffe; front row: Moyse, Henley. The only survivors from the pre-war Reading team were Deverall and MacPhee.

Ted Drake was the former Arsenal and England centre-forward appointed as Reading manager in June 1947. He stayed for five years and in his charge Reading were twice runners-up and once third at a time, unfortunately, when only one team was promoted from Division Three (South). Drake made many clever signings and also set up a highly successful youth scheme.

Left: Fred May was appointed as secretary in August 1947 and by the time of his retirement in 1978 he had served seven managers. His expertise and dedication steered the club through many crises and after his death the guests' room at Elm Park was named the 'Fred May Lounge' in his honour. *Right*: Maurice Edelston was one of the finest players ever to appear for Reading. He was an amateur international, played for the full England team in wartime and made a total of 223 league and cup appearances for Reading, the majority as captain, scoring 80 goals. After leaving football he became a BBC radio commentator.

Four

Division Three
Respectability
(1948–1971)

The Reading line-up for the home game against Southend United on 23 September 1950. From left to right, back row: Kinsell, Brice, Bewley, Marks, Wicks, Moyse; front row: Simpson, Johnston, Dodgin (captain), Brooks, Parker.

Pre-season training in the late 1940s and early 1950s took a fairly casual form, and lapping and sprinting were mixed with leisurely pursuits such as games of rounders on the Elm Park pitch

Some of the 17,185 people who saw the Reading v. Dartford F.A. Cup-tie on Saturday. Reading won 4-0, and meet Newport away on January 6 in the third round of the competition.
(1951)

Crowds were quite relaxed as well, and there was no segregation between the Reading and Dartford supporters who watched an FA Cup second-round game between the two teams in December 1950. A total of 17,185 saw Reading beat the non-leaguers 4–0.

Reading had to borrow a set of shirts from Portsmouth FC for an FA Cup second-round second replay against Southport at the neutral venue of Villa Park in December 1951. Simpson (left) and Edelston watch a shot from Henley beat the goalkeeper in the club's 2–0 victory.

In the following round, in January 1952, Reading lost 3–0 to Swansea Town at Elm Park. Marks, Johnston, Lewis, Wicks, and Brice are all helpless to prevent the Welsh club's first goal.

Before the Reading versus Millwall league match at Elm Park on 9 February 1952, both teams and spectators paid their respects to King George VI, who had died three days earlier.

Reading finished as runners-up in Division Three (South) in 1951–52, but the reserve team went one better, winning the Football Combination championship by beating Spurs reserves 4–0 at Elm Park in April 1952. From left to right, back row: Fisher, Amor, Barton, McBride, Livingstone, Street, McLean; front row: Farquhar, Hodges, Owens, Parker, Brooks.

The Reading players who achieved such success at first- and reserve-team level during the 1951–52 season. From left to right, back row: Leach, McLean, Owens, Vigar, Livingstone, Wicks, Brice, Lewis, Smith, Farquhar; middle row: Penny (groundstaff), Robson (trainer), Hodges, Marks, Kirkwood, McBride, Barton, Oxberry (trainer), Davidson (coach); front row: May (secretary), Fisher, Hutton, Simpson, Street, Edelston, Lee (chairman), Henley, Blackman, Johnston, Parker, Bainbridge, Drake (manager).

Bill Parker only scored six league goals for Reading, but this is one of them, the first of the 1952–53 season in a 2–0 win against Leyton Orient at Elm Park.

Ron Blackman (hoops) scores against Colchester United in a 2–0 win on 3 September 1952. He holds the record for most goals scored in league games for Reading, with a total of 156 from 228 appearances between 1946 and 1954.

Even reserve-team matches drew a fair sprinkling of supporters to Elm Park during the 1950s. Reading's reserve team had been elected to the Football Combination in 1926 and remained in that competition until 1992.

Typical scenes from a first-team game at Elm Park in the early 1950s, when attendances averaged over 15,000. The two photographs were taken for Sutton & Sons Ltd, who were responsible for maintaining the playing surface during the summer months.

Jack Smith was appointed Reading manager during the summer of 1952 and stayed for just over three years. On his arrival at Elm Park he was welcomed by Mr Bill Lee, the club's managing director, and Ted Drake, his predecessor. Nowadays, such pleasantries are rarely observed between incoming and outgoing managers!

The Reading players at the beginning of the 1953–54 season, their second under new manager Jack Smith. From left to right, back row: Robshaw, Reeves, J. Wicks, S. Wicks, Livingstone, Blackman, Quinlan, Docherty; middle row: Wallbanks (trainer), Robson (assistant trainer), Simpson, Smith, Hall, Jones, Davis, Leach, Davidson (coach), Marks (coach); front row: Uphill, Grieve, Ritchie, Kirkwood, Coulson, McCall, Hampson, Hinshelwood.

WELCOME TO READING

by TOM JACKSON of the "MANCHESTER EVENING NEWS"

Worthy representatives of southern football, Reading come to Old Trafford this afternoon fully deserving the right to contest their third-round F.A. Cup-tie with United for the second time. Their achievement in earning a replay, after a 1-1 draw at Elm Park last Saturday, was one of the best performances by a Third Division club against senior rivals.

To-day's replay brings Reading to Old Trafford for the first time for eighteen years. Their last visit was also in the third round of the Cup in 1937 when centre-forward Tommy Bamford won the match for United with a goal four minutes from time.

These were the teams:

United: Breen; Vose, Roughton; Brown, Winterbottom, Whalley; Bryant, Mutch, Bamford, McKay, Lang.

Reading: Whittaker; Gregory, Robson; Johnson, Hayhurst, Wright; Watkin, Glidden, Tait, Paterson, Fielding.

Altogether United and Reading have contested five Cup-ties since 1911 and have had to replay four times. In 1926-7 the clubs clashed three times before Reading won through to round four with a 2-1 victory at Villa Park.

Reading team personalities:

David Meeson (goalkeeper).
Son of a former Arsenal and England amateur international goalkeeper. Was signed from Wolves last August, but first came to notice with Oxford City. Aged twenty-one and shows fine promise.

Dennis Penford (full-back).
One of several "locals" in the side. Became a professional at Elm Park after coming to the fore in junior football and has made a big impression at right back this season.

Brian Leach (full-back).
Hails from Pangbourne, near Reading, and another player recruited from local junior circles. Missed only one league game last term and is equally at home in the half-back line.

Fred Davis (wing half-back).
Formerly with Bloxwich Strollers, a Midlands junior club, and is a native of Walsall. Has shown good constructive ideas at right-half this season and has missed few senior games.

Bill Livingstone (centre half-back).
A Scot who marked his come-back after injury with a strong display last Saturday. Has frequently led the attack, but came to the rescue when Ray Reeves, the regular pivot, was injured.

Eddie McLaren (wing half-back).
Another Scot who has made his mark in the Reading side. Had a spell with Wolves before moving south two seasons ago and now completes a strong middle line.

Dennis Simpson (outside-right).
In his fifth year at Elm Park, having been signed from Coventry City, where he has developed as a junior. Is a brainy type of player who has "teamed" well with Hinshelwood on the right wing. Born at Coventry.

Wally Hinshelwood (inside-right).
A Londoner who made his league debut for Fulham in 1948-9 and later had a spell with Chelsea before returning to Fulham. Since joining Reading has made a hit as a marksman and forward schemer. Is very fast.

Bobby Campbell (centre-forward).
Captain of the team and a Scottish international winger signed from Chelsea last August. Has played a big part in Reading's successes since being switched to the middle. Was a war-time discovery by Falkirk.

Dennis Uphill (inside-left).
Also recruited from a London club. Joined Reading from Spurs two years ago and has proved another real asset. Born at Bath and has played for the Army in representative soccer. Introduced to league football by Spurs in 1950 as a junior.

Barry Mansell (outside-left).
Signed from Portsmouth as a left-back at the end of last season when he made his league debut. Was switched to outside-left for the first tie with United and made a good impression. Born at Portsmouth and a discovery from the Forces.

Jimmy Wheeler (outside-left).
A nineteen-year-old signing from Reading junior football. Made only three league appearances last season, but continues to be one of the most promising juniors on the club's books. Was twelfth man for the first tie at Elm Park.

SCOREBOARD KEY, WEDNESDAY, 12th JAN., 1955
F.A., CUP, THIRD ROUND REPLAYS

A	B. A'land v. Ipswich	D	Liverpool v. L'coln C.
B	B'ford C. v. Brentford	E	Stoke City v. Bury
C	D'gton v. H'pools U.	F	Torquay v. Leeds U.

Edited by SIDNEY F. WICKS LTD., 21 Newton Street, Manchester 1. CENtral 9047
Printed at the Philips Park Press by C. NICHOLLS & COMPANY LTD.

Reading's best performance under Jack Smith was to hold a Manchester United team packed with internationals to a 1–1 draw in an FA Cup third-round tie at Elm Park on 8 January 1955. The programme for the replay at Old Trafford included pen-portraits of the Reading players, as well as references to previous ties between the two clubs.

Reading were well beaten in the replay at Manchester United by four goals to one. The white-shirted Reading players (from left to right: Leach, McLaren, Livingstone, Davis, goalkeeper Meeson, Penford, and Campbell) try in vain to prevent the fourth Manchester goal.

PREPARING FOR A HARVEST OF GOALS.—Close-season activity at Elm Park, where, following the laying of a new drainage system, the pitch is now being ploughed, harrowed

A new drainage system was installed at Elm Park during the summer of 1955. Groundsman Bill Smith drives the tractor as the pitch is ploughed, harrowed, and levelled prior to reseeding. The floodlights along the roof of the stand were put in place in October 1954, and not replaced until 1969.

Areff's cartoon in the *Berkshire Chronicle* highlighted the goalkeeping display by David Jones in the 2–2 draw against Norwich City at Elm Park in September 1955. Jones played 215 league games for Reading between 1953 and 1961, and was included in the Welsh international squad for the 1958 World Cup finals in Sweden.

Reading nearly had to seek re-election at the end of the 1955–56 season, but a series of dour defensive displays, including this 0–0 draw at Swindon, avoided that embarrassment. Goalkeeper David Jones saves a shot inches from goal, covered by (from left to right) Reeves, McLaren, Leach, Spiers, and Penford.

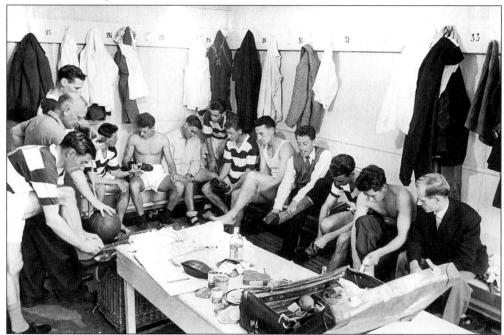

September 1957 and the Reading team get stripped for action in the changing room at Crystal Palace. From left to right: Campbell, Wallbanks (trainer), Dixon, Goodall, Jones, Evans, Gunning, Wheeler, Reeves, Anderton, Spiers, Webb, and Harrison (twelfth man). The trainer's medical bag had clearly doubled as a suitcase on several holidays!

A little later that same September afternoon and a policeman behind the goal has a close-up view of Douggie Webb scoring Reading's second goal in the 2–2 draw at Selhurst Park.

Douggie Webb (centre) and Tommy Dixon (right) watch a shot from Peter Harrison beat the Crystal Palace goalkeeper in a 2–2 draw at Elm Park on 8 February 1958. This was to be Reading's last season in Division Three (South) as they joined the non-regional Third Division at the start of the following season. The section of the 'Simonds' advert in the South Bank roof had been removed to accommodate television cameras.

Members of the Reading FC Supporters' Club are joined by directors and their wives for a dinner at the Co-operative Restaurant on 21 March 1958. Chairman A.E. Smith is fourth from the right, and on his right is secretary, Fred May.

THE READING FOOTBALL CLUB
Founded 1871   LIMITED

Members of the Football Association, Berks and Bucks Football Association, The Football League
Football Combination, Hampshire League, Reading & District Football League & Reading Minor League

Directors:
Chairman—Mr. E. J. Carter   *Vice-Chairman*—Mr. A. E. Smith
Mr. A. E. Perris   Mr. F. V. Waller   Mr. J. S. Windebank

Registered Office:

Telephone and Telegrams
READING 54154   **ELM PARK, NORFOLK RD.,**   *Team Manager:* H. Johnston

READING   *Secretary:* F. May

April 30th, 1957.

Mr. D. Webb

Dear Sir,

I beg to inform you that your services have been retained by the above Club for season 1957-58, and I am instructed to offer you the following terms:---

Playing Season, £....8.... per week, plus £....2.... extra when playing in the First Team.

Non-Playing Season, £.....6.... per week.

May I take this opportunity of thanking you for your past services to the Club and to wish you well in the future.

Yours faithfully,

[signature]

Secretary.

Left: a letter received by Douggie Webb telling him that he had been retained by Reading FC for another season. The letter that every player dreaded receiving began: 'I regret to inform you that the Club has decided not …'. *Right*: players often supplemented their summer wages by helping with maintenance work around the ground. Jimmy Whitehouse (left) and Bill Livingstone assist groundsman Bill Smith to concrete the banking at the Tilehurst End in 1958.

Another goal for Douggie Webb (left) as he nets the decider in a 3–2 win against Barnsley on 30 December 1959. The inside-forward scored 81 Football League goals for Reading between 1956 and 1967 and is also the club's record reserve-team scorer with a total of 106 in Football Combination matches.

Jimmy Whitehouse (left) slots home Reading's third goal in a 5–1 victory over Torquay United on 29 April 1961. Reading had an excellent home record in the 1960–61 season, but could only finish eighteenth in Division Three after winning just one game away from home.

Reading manager Harry Johnston was a great believer in the club's youth policy throughout his stay at Elm Park from 1955 to 1962 and he was delighted when the youth team won an international tournament in Germany. Johnston (left) admires the trophy held by Reading and England youth international David High while also looking on are coach Bobby Campbell and trainer Jimmy Wallbanks.

Skipper Johnny Walker, followed by goalkeeper Meeson, Spiers, and Goodall, leads out the Reading team for the league game at Lincoln City on 9 December 1961, a match Reading won 2–0. Walker was an inspirational captain and played 287 league matches for Reading between 1957 and 1965.

The following Saturday Reading were also away but forgot to pack a change strip for the fixture at Coventry City. Their line-up for the game, wearing Coventry's own change colours with the white collar and cuffs hidden, was, from left to right, back row: Spiers, Goodall, Meeson, High, Evans; front row: Wheeler, Whitehouse, Walker, Lacey, Webb, Allen. Reading could not repeat their success at Lincoln, losing 1–0.

Reading lost 1–0 at home to Bournemouth in April 1962, despite an almost continual bombardment of the visitors' goal. Lacey and Wheeler (10) challenge for the ball but are outnumbered by a packed Bournemouth defence. Reading finished in a typically respectable seventh place in Division Three that season.

Reading goalkeeper Arthur Wilkie set a Football League record on 31 August 1962 by scoring twice in a 4–2 home win against Halifax Town. He had moved to an outfield position after injuring his back making a save. Areff's cartoon in the *Berkshire Chronicle* told the full story of an unusual game.

Roy Bentley replaced Harry Johnston as Reading manager in January 1963. Like Johnston and Drake he was an England international and stayed at Reading for six years, often taking the club close to promotion. He is standing in the centre of his board of directors. From left to right: W.T.D. Vincent, L. Davies, F.V. Waller, Bentley, A.E. Smith (chairman), F. May (secretary), D.P. Baylis.

The winter 'freeze-up' of 1962–63 meant the abandonment of Reading's Boxing Day match against Bristol Rovers, and the postponement of fixtures throughout January and February. Groundsman Bill Smith faced a hopeless task as he tried to clear the Elm Park pitch of snow.

Pre-season training 1964-style as manager Bentley (in tracksuit) supervises his players, some of whom have just finished lapping the track while the remainder practise their heading.

The Reading squad at the start of the 1965–66 season wearing the new sky-blue strip. From left to right, back row: Neate, Travers, Fairchild, Wilkie, Silvester, Rusher, Dean; middle row: Scarrott, Webb, Bayliss, Norton, Lacey (trainer); front row: Maidment, P. Knight, McDonald, Wheeler, Hollidge, B. Knight, Faulkes.

A goalmouth scramble in an FA Cup tie against Brentford on 7 December 1965 which Reading won 5–0. Pat Terry (centre), supported by Webb and Allen, challenges the goalkeeper for a high ball. The photograph was used as the programme cover for the following season, hence the '1966–7' logo.

Left: Jimmy Wheeler played over 400 first-team games for Reading and scored 144 league goals. Towards the end of this career he was appointed assistant manager, and captained the reserve team to the Football Combination Division Two championship. Over 6,000 watched a 1–1 draw with Bournemouth reserves on 25 May 1966, a result which clinched the title and brought Reading the shield. *Right*: Maurice Evans also played in excess of 400 first-team games for the club, and his skill at wing-half made him one of the most popular players ever to wear a Reading shirt. He was also universally recognised as one of the game's true gentlemen. He played for Reading between 1955 and 1967, was coach from 1974 until 1977, then managed the club from 1977 until 1984.

Goalkeeper Mike Dixon was elected 'player of the season' for 1967–68 by Reading supporters. It was a remarkable achievement by the former England schoolboy international as he had been a reserve until November and was also a part-timer, training in the evenings with the amateur players. His main occupation was as manager of a newsagent's shop in Tilehurst.

Reading played in a rather flashy sky-blue kit between 1965 and 1969 instead of the traditional blue and white hoops, but the new strip was never really popular with the fans. Players Ernie Yard (left), John Chapman and Dick Spiers display the new style during a 1–1 draw with Oxford United in February 1968.

After retiring from full-time football through injury, Douggie Webb (centre) was presented with a farewell cheque by chairman Frank Waller in November 1969. The ceremony took place in the dressing room before a 2–1 home win over Mansfield Town. The Reading players looking on are, from left to right: Dean, Spiers, Brown, Harris, Allen, Thornhill, Chapman, Sainty, and Silvester.

Gordon Neate (hoops, left) played for Reading in the 1960s, though he did not usually get as far forward as this, most of his 99 league appearances being at full-back. After leaving the game through injury, he became the Elm Park groundsman, a post he still holds. In 1996 he was presented with the Football League Long Service Award after completing forty years at the club.

Jack Mansell took over as Reading manager in April 1969 and was reported to be earning the 'vast sum' of £100 a week. He encouraged an attacking style of play and at the end of his first full season Reading qualified for the Watney Cup as the leading scorers in Division Three.

The floodlights on the roof of the Elm Park stands were replaced during the summer of 1969. Four 100ft pylons were hoisted in by crane at each corner of the ground, at a total cost of £22,696.

An unfortunate injury occurred during Reading's 1–0 win against Rochdale at Elm Park on 28 February 1970. The visitors' striker, Tony Buck (left) had his leg grotesquely broken in an accidental collision with Reading keeper, Steve Death.

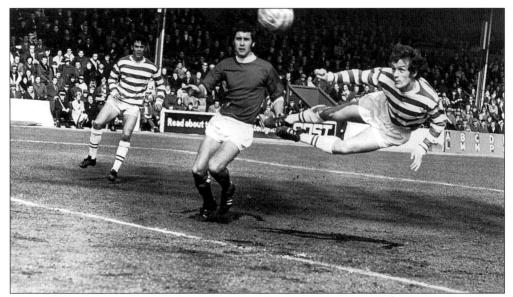

One of the most spectacular goals ever seen at Elm Park as Les Campbell, admired by Gordon Cumming, glides through the air to complete this hat-trick in the 6–3 win against Barnsley on 4 April 1970.

The Reading squad line up for a team picture before a match in the 1969–70 season. From left to right, back row: Stuart Morgan, Barrie Wagstaff, Denis Allen, Steve Death, Wilf Dixon, Denis Butler, Fred Sharpe; front row: Gordon Cumming, Terry Bell, Les Chappell, John Harley, Dick Habbin, Tony Wagstaff, Bobby Williams.

The Watney Cup match against Manchester United in August 1970 was one of the most exciting games seen at Elm Park for many years. Reading were beaten 3–2, but played encouragingly. Their goals came from Gordon Cumming and Dick Habbin (above), who volleyed home from close range.

Jack Mansell's time as manager came to an end in 1971 as Reading were relegated to Division Four in the club's centenary year. Only fourteen league games were won in 1970–71, including a 2–1 victory against Port Vale on 1 November 1970. But the game was a farce with players from both teams sending up sprays of water as they tried to play on a waterlogged pitch.

Denis Allen (right) was a very popular Reading player throughout the 1960s and early 1970s. He was signed from Charlton Athletic for just £900, and proved excellent value for money. He made almost 350 appearances for the club, scoring 85 league goals, many of them from free kicks. He played in almost every position, including emergency goalkeeper, and was rewarded with a testimonial in 1970. He later played for Bournemouth, then managed Cheltenham Town.

Five
Ups and Downs
(1971–1984)

Charlie Hurley took over as manager during the 1971–72 season and the former Eire international's first meeting with his players took place in Prospect Park. Hurley (second from left) is greeted by, from left to right: Wallbanks (trainer), Wagstaff, Archer, Swain, Harley, Flannigan, Morgan, Dixon, Wooler, James, Cooper, Harman, and Chappell.

Hurley's first game in charge of the team was an FA Cup third-round replay at home to amateur side Blyth Spartans. Played on a Wednesday afternoon, the tie attracted a crowd of 10,550, which saw Reading win 6–1. Peter Harman (centre) scored this second goal for Reading and completed a hat-trick during the match.

Barry Wagstaff jumps to head Reading's first goal in a 2–0 victory over Aldershot at Elm Park in January 1972. Reading completed the double over their local rivals that season as well as knocking them out of the FA Cup. However, Reading's final position of sixteenth in Division Four remains their lowest placing in the Football League.

Reading's best post-war FA Cup run was in 1972–73 when they drew 1–1 in the fourth round with Sunderland, the eventual winners, at Roker Park. Les Chappell (8), supported by John Hulme, is seen here heading Reading into an early lead. Reading lost the replay 3–1.

When the charismatic Robin Friday scored a last-minute winner in a 2–1 win over Rochdale at Elm Park on 9 April 1975, he celebrated by running behind the goal and kissing the policeman. The home fans and colleague John Ashton, as well as the policeman, seemed to approve of the gesture.

An unusual incident happened during the first match of the 1975–76 season. A free kick by Reading's Tommy Youlden hit the outside of the Rochdale net and their goalkeeper placed the ball for a goal kick. However, referee Walter Harvey ran up to collect the ball and inform the goalkeeper that he had awarded a goal. The incident will always be remembered as 'the goal that never was'. Reading won the game 2–0.

Reading drew 1–1 against Lincoln City, the eventual champions, in this Division Four match at Elm Park on 10 April 1976. The highest crowd of the season, 15,683, saw Ray Hiron (right) head Reading's goal.

Reading's drew 2–2 at Cambridge United in April 1976 to ensure promotion to Division Three. Robin Friday (9) starts to celebrate after scoring his team's first goal.

On the final day of the 1975–76 season Reading beat Crewe Alexandra 3–1 to finish in third place in Division Four. Dennis Nelson (hoops) scored the third goal in the last minute.

The crowd streamed onto the pitch after the last game of the 1975–76 season to celebrate, and with some justification – it was the first time Reading had gained promotion for fifty years.

Reading made the short journey to Loakes Park, the home of Isthmian League Wycombe Wanderers, for an FA Cup second-round match in December 1976. Robin Friday (centre) scored both Reading's goals and here he slips the second past an off-balance Wanderers' defence.

Reading's return to Division Three only lasted one season and former player Maurice Evans replaced Hurley in 1977 to become the club's eighth post-war manager. He had previously been manager of Shrewsbury Town and coach under Hurley at Elm Park.

Elm Park was still the club's home when Evans took over as manager, and had another 21 years of its existence to come. By now, however, it was hemmed in by housing on all sides and parking at home games was causing problems for local residents.

Fred May finally retired from Reading FC in October 1977. At his retirement dinner he was presented with an engraved salver by Alan Hardaker, secretary of the Football League. Attending the presentation were, from left to right: Mrs May, Frank Waller (club chairman), Mr May, Mrs Waller, Mrs Hardaker, Mr Hardaker.

One shot that goalkeeper Steve Death need not have dived for was this penalty kick sent wide by an Aldershot player in the FA Cup tie at Elm Park on 26 November 1977. Reading won the match 3–1 but lost at non-league Wealdstone in the next round.

Midfield player Richie Bowman was voted Reading's 'player of the season' for 1977–78 and was presented with the trophy in front of his team-mates who are, from left to right: Davies, Bennett, Turner, White, Lewis, Hicks, Earles, Nelson, Peters, and Williams.

A feature of Maurice Evans's time as Reading manager was his encouragement of local schools' football. He would frequently take coaching sessions with youngsters, like this one with the Reading Primary Schools squad in 1978. The lads are, from left to right: Jonathan Bartlett, Douglas Seeburg, Andrew Fitzpatrick, Paul Dixon, Stuart Neate, Anthony House, Andrew Parr, Lee Povey, Andrew Jupp, Matthew Webb, and Adam Hartley.

Reading began the 1978–79 season brightly with a 2–1 win away to Grimsby on the opening day. Pat Earles (centre) scored the first goal with this close-range finish then Ollie Kearns (right) got the second before half-time.

Maurice Evans leads his players on a lap of honour round Elm Park after a 1–0 win against Wimbledon in May 1979. It was the last home game of a season in which Reading won the Division Four championship.

Reading clinched the Fourth Division title with a 3–0 win away to Port Vale on 5 May 1979. The first goal was scored by Martin Hicks (*above*), who volleyed the ball home after four minutes, with Steve Hetzke (9) watching. Pat Earles (*below*, centre) side-footed the second in the fifty-eighth minute.

Reading's third goal at Port Vale came from John Alexander (*above*) who made the game safe in the sixty-second minute. The players left the muddy pitch (*below*) in a relaxed mood knowing that they had not only won the title but also set a Football League record by not conceding a goal for eleven matches. Ready for a well-deserved shower and drink in the bar are, from left to right: Sanchez, Hicks, Death, White, Earles, and Bennett.

Open days gave supporters the chance to watch the players train in preparation for the new season. At this one in August 1979 a youthful Neil Webb jogs past the Division Four trophy and championship flag.

Left: goalkeeper Steve Death is presented with his Division Four championship plaque by chairman, Frank Waller. Death played over 500 first-team games for Reading and was four times voted 'player of the season'. He holds the Football League record of 1,103 minutes without conceding a goal. *Right*: the less glamorous side of a footballer's life was experienced by John Alexander, who was carried off after breaking his leg in a match at Brentford in November 1979. Reading drew the game 2–2 but the injury signified the end of Alexander's career with the club.

A well-deserved moment of relaxation for goalkeeper Death, who had a double reason for celebrating his testimonial game against a Young England XI on 14 November 1979. Not only had he kept another clean sheet in Reading's 1–0 victory but the attendance of 7,500 meant he could expect a cheque for £10,000 from that game. Sitting next to Death is Wayne Wanklyn, a non-playing substitute that evening.

The Reading squad for the 1979–80 season was, from left to right, back row: Lewis, Moreline, Webb, Alexander, Williams, Bennett; middle row: Evans (manager), Peters, Kearns, Sanchez, Hetzke, Hicks, Kearney, White, Wallbanks (physio); front row: Henderson (player/coach), Cullen, Earles, Death, Wanklyn, Bowman, Webb (assistant physio)

The first Reading team to take three points in a league match was the one which beat Doncaster Rovers 1–0 away from home on the opening day of the 1981–82 season. The points system had been changed but Reading looked likely to fail to take advantage until Pat Earles (centre) headed an injury-time winner.

The local derby between Reading and Swindon at Elm Park on 20 February 1982 was remarkable for the fact that both goals in a 1–1 draw were own goals scored by each team's goalkeeper. Neil Webb (centre) celebrates as his challenge causes the opposing keeper to fumble the ball into his own net.

Webb, who had just returned from the England Youth tour to Australia, was on the mark again, scoring from the penalty spot in a 2–1 win against Wimbledon. He finished the 1981–82 season as the club's leading scorer with fifteen goals.

The lowest crowd to watch a league match at Elm Park was the 1,713 which saw Reading lose 3–2 against Preston North End on 2 October 1982. Reading slumped to the bottom of Division Three as a result of that defeat and immediately afterwards the board of directors put the club up for sale.

A reunion of former players was held at Elm Park before the game against Walsall in March 1983. Those who watched a 1–1 draw and who must have longed for the days of all-out attack were, from left to right: Jimmy Whitehouse, Bernard Goodall, Colin Meldrum, Len Vallard, Mike Dixon, Douggie Webb, Bill Lacey, Jimmy Wheeler, David Jones, Ray Reeves, Johnny Walker, Denis Allen, and Ron Blackman.

CASH OFFER

by

HENRY ANSBACHER & CO. LIMITED

on behalf of

ROBERT MAXWELL, M.C.

to acquire the whole of the issued ordinary share capital of

THE READING FOOTBALL CLUB PLC

other than the 9,122 ordinary shares already owned by Mr. Maxwell

The procedure for acceptance is set out on page 8.

The Offer will close at 3.30 p.m. on 6th July, 1983.

In June 1983 Robert Maxwell made an attempt to buy a controlling interest in Reading FC. His plan was to merge the club with Oxford United and form a new team to be called Thames Valley Royals. His takeover bid was defeated by shareholders, however, and a new Reading FC board, consisting of Roger Smee (chairman), Jim Brooks, Roy Tranter, and Richard Cox, was elected.

Two members of the new board were Roy Tranter (*left*) a former vice-president and long-time supporter of the club, and Roger Smee (*right*), who had played first-team football for Reading between 1967 and 1970.

The Reading line-up for the 1983–84 season was, from left to right, back row: Williams, Wood, Senior, Barnes, Judge, Hicks, Sanchez, Horrix; front row: Beavon, Price, White, Tutty, Crown, Richardson. The team was beginning the campaign in Division Four after relegation from the Third.

Reading players celebrate a goal by Wayne Tutty (centre) in the 3–2 win against Doncaster Rovers at Elm Park in September 1983. The club was later banned from wearing the shirts with the Radio 210 logo on the front because, it was claimed, the numerals might be confusing to referees!

Reading regained their Division Three place after just one season, ending 1983–84 in third place. Promotion was ensured in the final home match with this long-range free kick by Mark White eluding the Tranmere Rovers goalkeeper to bring Reading a 1–0 win.

The crowd came onto the pitch after the Tranmere game and the players appeared in the directors' box to acknowledge their supporters. Midfielder Lawrie Sanchez, with Stuart Beavon behind him, turns to face the camera.

Six

Finals and Finale
(1984–1997)

The Reading first-team squad for the 1984–85 season. From left to right, back row: Glenn Hunter (physio), Jerry Williams, Ken Price, Steve Wood, Trevor Senior, Martin Hicks, Lawrie Sanchez, Dean Horrix, Colin Duncan, Stewart Henderson (coach); front row: Stuart Beavon, Michael Gilkes, Mark White, Gary Westwood, Ian Branfoot (manager), Alan Judge, Derrick Christie, David Crown, Steve Richardson.

The 1985–86 season began in spectacular fashion as Reading set a Football League record by winning the first thirteen games. Jerry Williams jumped to head the only goal of the opening fixture, a 1–0 victory against Blackpool at Elm Park on 17 August 1985.

Crowds built up slowly during 1985–86, from the 3,190 who watched the Blackpool game to the 12,266 who saw Reading beat Derby County to make certain of the championship in April. Executive boxes had been built in the main grandstand but the terracing behind the Tilehurst goal was still packed with die-hard fans.

Reading made history with their twelfth consecutive league win at Newport County on 12 October 1985. Goals from Stuart Beavon (*above*) and Kevin Bremner (*below*) brought Reading a 2–0 victory in front of a crowd of 6,449, of whom 4,000 were estimated to be travelling Reading supporters.

The president of the Football League, Jack Dunnett, visited Reading to present chairman, Roger Smee, with an engraved salver to commemorate the club's achievement in establishing a new League record.

In November 1985 Reading's squad of associate schoolboys were each presented with a sports hold-all and club tie by members of the Vice-Presidents' Club, led by Alan Finch (left). Four of the youngsters – George Friel, Andrew King, Scott Taylor, and Adrian Williams – went on to play for Reading's first team.

When Reading played at Blackpool in January 1986 manager Branfoot took his team for a training run along the front before the game. The tactic worked, as Reading came away with another valuable point after a 0–0 draw.

The low point of the 1985–86 season was when winger Andy Rogers fell heavily on a bone-hard pitch at Swansea and stopped breathing. His life was saved by physio Glenn Hunter, who inserted an airway into his throat. Reading players Peters, Hicks, and Beavon look on as the drama unfolds. Happily, Rogers made a complete recovery and was playing again within three weeks.

Striker Dean Horrix never missed a penalty for Reading and this one produced the second goal in a 2–0 win against Bury at Elm Park during the race for the title.

Reading needed to draw away to Darlington on 19 April 1986 to be sure of promotion to Division Two. Eight supporters made certain of being there by chartering an aeroplane from Blackbushe Airport to fly north. They were, from left to right: Colin Shaxted, Steve Goulding, Steve Raybould, Glen Hall, Keith Harbor, Simon Eedle, Trevor Miles, and Rodney Stimpson. Their dedication was rewarded with a 0–0 result.

The final game of the 1985–86 season was played in a carnival atmosphere at home to Doncaster Rovers although the team was in no mood to relax. Trevor Senior, who totalled 31 goals for the season, added this tap-in to an earlier volley as Reading won 2–0 in front of a crowd of 8,168.

When Reading were presented with the Canon League trophy as Division Three champions, they invited 89-year-old Frank Richardson to join them in the Elm Park centre-circle. He had played centre-forward for the last Reading team to win the Division Three title, sixty years previously in 1926.

As part of the 1986 championship celebrations, Reading players and staff were taken to a reception and guided tour at the Houses of Parliament by the two members for Reading, Tony Durant (Reading West) and Sir Gerry Vaughan (Reading East).

Reading continued to develop their links with the community by holding a series of soccer schools during the summer of 1986. Over 300 youngsters attended the schools, which were staffed by players from the club and local schoolteachers.

Winning Division Three meant that Reading were exempt until the third round of the following season's FA Cup competition. Captain Martin Hicks needed plenty of support from his mascots when he shook hands with Arsenal's Kenny Sansom before the tie.

Reading lost 3–1 to their First Division opponents on 10 January 1987, with the only bright spot for the home fans being this headed goal by Trevor Senior. A crowd of 16,822 watched the tie, which set a new receipts record for Elm Park of £71,000.

Reading players were required to take part in a publicity stunt for the Post Office in October 1986. From left to right: Stuart Beavon, Kevin Bremner, Paul Canoville, Gary Westwood, Terry Hurlock, and Martin Hicks wore the Elm Park postcode to remind fans that Reading now had a mechanised letter office, and that postcodes should be used on all letters. The slogan associated with the campaign was 'Royals reign over RG3 2EF'.

Reading finished the 1986–87 season in thirteenth place in Division Two, the club's highest placing in the Football League. The last game of the campaign was an exciting 1–1 draw away to Ipswich Town, where Reading's point was protected through this acrobatic save by goalkeeper Steve Francis.

Unfortunately Reading's stay in Division Two only lasted two seasons. A scrambled goal by Billy Whitehurst (fourth from left) brought a much-needed 2–1 win against Barnsley on 9 April 1988 but the team was in deep trouble at the time and remained in twenty-second position in the division.

The league programme for 1987–88 ended in despair for Reading as a 0–0 home draw against Hull City in the final match meant relegation to Division Three. Bloodied Martin Hicks was inconsolable as he left the pitch at the end of the game.

1987–88 was, despite relegation, the season which contained the club's greatest triumph. Reading beat four Division One teams on the way to Wembley and the final of the Simod Cup. In the semi-final Reading knocked out Coventry City after a penalty shoot-out. Steve Francis (*above*) saved two of the five spot-kicks aimed at his goal, then Michael Gilkes (*below*) converted to take his team through to Wembley. Gilkes's match-winning penalty was scored at 10.45pm, the latest-ever finish to a match at Elm Park.

Fans queued for hours to buy tickets for the Simod Cup final, with supporters lining Norfolk Road to wait for their chance at the turnstiles. Of the crowd of 61,740 which saw the final against Luton Town, it was estimated that 40,000 came from Reading.

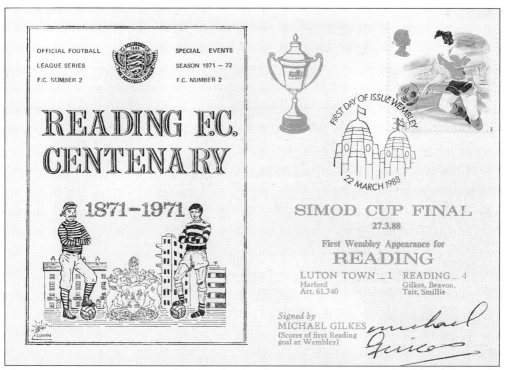

This commemorative cover marked Reading's achievement in winning the Simod Cup. The covers had first been produced on the occasion of the club's centenary in 1971 and were overprinted with details of the Wembley final and signed by goalscorer Michael Gilkes.

The greatest day in the history of Reading FC is, in many people's minds, 27 March 1988, when the team beat Luton Town 4–1 at Wembley to win the Simod Cup, a competition open to First and Second Division clubs. *Above*: Michael Gilkes turns in triumph after scoring Reading's first and equalising goal. *Below*: every Reading player is in the picture as Stuart Beavon gives his team the lead from the penalty spot.

Skipper Martin Hicks holds the Simod Cup aloft in the royal box, followed by Beavon, Keith Curle, and Steve Richardson.

The Reading goalscorers at Wembley celebrate with the trophy and their medals after the final. From left to right: Gilkes, Mick Tait, Beavon, and Neil Smillie.

Martin Hicks was presented with a glass decanter by chairman Roger Smee and director Michael King to mark his 500th first-team appearance on Boxing Day 1989. Hicks holds the appearance record for the club with 577 first-team games between 1978 and 1991.

Also honoured was Trevor Senior, who was given a golden boot by King and fellow director John Campbell on 2 October 1990. He had scored his 167th goal for Reading, thereby surpassing Ron Blackman's record which had stood for thirty-six years.

Mark McGhee was appointed Reading manager in May 1991. A former Scottish international, he continued playing until 1993 and was close to scoring with this effort against Hull City in September 1992.

Welsh international Adrian Williams set an unusual Football League record when he wore the No 10 shirt against Wrexham on 5 March 1994. It meant that he had worn every possible shirt number for the club, including those of substitute and replacement goalkeeper. He achieved this landmark at the age of only twenty-two.

Jimmy Quinn scored a total of 37 goals in league and cup matches as Reading became champions of Division Two in 1993–94. This is just one of them, a header in the league match against Burnley on 21 August 1993, which Reading won 2–1.

Order of Events

Saturday 26th February

10.00 am	Branch AGM
1.00 pm	Branch Outing and Picinic
3.00 pm	Cambridge F.C. –v– Reading F.C.
7.00 pm	Annual Dinner – Lamb & Flag Hotel, Welney
12.00 midnight	Midnight Mass at "Soffits"

Sunday 27th February

8.00 am	Annual Breakfast
9.00 am	Golf Tournament (Rear Paddock)
11.00 am	6-a-Side Competition (Garden)
1.00 pm	Lunch and Plenary Session

Menu Card sponsored by
Fericon Press Ltd of Reading
By Appointment: Printers to the Aristocracy

Reading F.C. Supporters' Club

EAST ANGLIAN BRANCH

Annual Dinner,
6-a-Side Competition
&
Golf Tournament

26th – 27th February 1994
at
Branch H.Q., Elm, Cambridgeshire

The East Anglian branch of the Reading Supporters' Club organises a weekend get-together once a season, usually timed to coincide with a Reading match in the area. The 1994 gathering had a varied programme, including an outing to the Division Two match at Cambridge United, won 1–0 by Reading.

114

Ball, match and kit sponsorship all became an important feature of the commercial department's money-raising activities during the 1980s and 1990s. For the home game against Port Vale in February 1994, the ball was sponsored by David Barr, a Reading supporter since the 1920s. He was presented with the ball after the game by skipper Mick Gooding.

Reading's final home game of the 1993–94 season was against Brighton when a 2–0 victory ensured the Division Two title would be coming to Elm Park. Quinn scored his second goal of the game in the last minute and the crowd streamed onto the pitch to begin the celebrations.

This cartoon was redrawn and amended by Bryan McAllister from his original in *The Guardian* for the author to mark Reading's Second Division championship success in 1994.

The Reading squad display the Division Two championship trophy on the *Auto Trader* stand at the 1994 Motor Show. From left to right, standing: Dylan Kerr, Phil Parkinson, Andy Bernal, Jimmy Quinn, Scott Taylor, Jeff Hopkins, Mick Gooding, Shaka Hislop, Adrian Williams, Daley Thompson; kneeling: Tom Jones, Mark McGhee (manager), John Madejski (chairman), Colin Lee (coach), Michael Gilkes. Olympic gold medallist Thompson had trained with the club and played in pre-season friendlies.

Before the home match with Bristol City on 15 October 1994, striker Jimmy Quinn was presented with a tankard by Colin Bishop (left) and Mike Habbitts of the Supporters' Club. It was to mark Quinn becoming the most capped player and most prolific international goalscorer in Reading's history. Quinn made a total of 17 appearances and scored 5 times for Northern Ireland during his career with Reading.

Two long-serving members of staff at Reading FC have been Bobby Williams (left) who played for the club between 1969 and 1971, then returned as youth-team coach from 1972 to 1997, and Gordon Neate (right), who played from 1958 to 1966 and, after a series of knee injuries ended his playing career, switched roles to become groundsman, a position he still holds in the final season at Elm Park.

After the departure of Mark McGhee, Reading turned to Jimmy Quinn (left) and Mick Gooding to take over the club as joint player/managers. Chairman John Madejski introduced the pair in their new roles in January 1995.

Centre-back Adrian Williams scored with this last-minute header to bring Reading a 2–1 win against Charlton Athletic on 7 May 1995. The victory gave Reading their highest-ever league placing, second in Division One, and ensured a play-off place against Tranmere Rovers.

The first leg of the play-off secured Reading's place at Wembley. Reading won 3–1 at Tranmere, with Stuart Lovell celebrating after scoring his own second and Reading's third goal. The second leg of the semi-final was a goalless draw and Reading were through to the play-off final against Bolton Wanderers.

The Reading team received incredible support from their fans at the Wembley play-off final. The attendance of 64,107, the largest to watch a Reading game, included the 36,500 who had bought all the tickets allocated to the club.

The Reading players congratulate striker Lee Nogan on his opening goal at Wembley. Reading were two goals ahead against Bolton Wanderers as they fought for a place in the Premier League, but eventually lost 4–3 after extra-time.

Reading players (from left to right) Hopkins, Gooding, Wdowczyk, Gilkes, and Osborne take a breather during the Wembley match. Although disappointed at their defeat, they could be proud of their efforts in taking part in one of the most exciting games seen at the national stadium.

Reading set yet another club record by reaching the quarter-finals of the League Cup competition in the 1995–96 season. They were fortunate in the third round when the home tie against Bury was abandoned with the visitors two goals ahead. But conditions were impossible as shown by the clash between former Reading striker Phil Stant (left) and Phil Parkinson. When the game was replayed Reading won 2–1.

A view from the Tilehurst End of a Reading–Ipswich Town game during the 1995–96 season. Although Reading were in the bottom half of the table for most of the season, and only made certain of avoiding relegation in the last home match, support remained good, with crowds averaging almost 9,000 at home games.

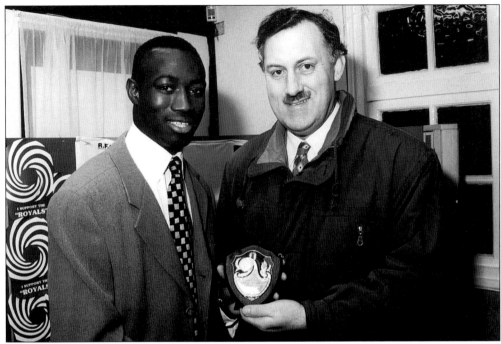

Centre-back Keith McPherson was presented with his 'player of the month' award for January 1997 by Clive Baskerville, a sports reporter with the *Evening Post* who covers Reading's matches. The award is sponsored jointly by the *Post* and Astres Trophies of Tilehurst.

The *Evening Post* also gave fans the opportunity to speak their mind about the team's performance via the 'Fan's Verdict' column published after each game. Two loyal supporters who were regularly featured in the column were Denny Fullbrook (*left*), the Supporters' Club travel organiser, and Tommy Bartholemew (*right*), Supporters' Club committee member and organiser of social events for many years.

A dinner was held on 5 September 1996 to commemorate the exact centenary of the opening of Elm Park. Among the guests were, from left to right, back row: Gordon Neate (groundsman), Frank Orton (president), John Madejski (chairman), David Downs (historian); front row: Roy Bentley (former manager and secretary), Jimmy Quinn and Mick Gooding (joint player/managers), Maurice Evans (former manager), Jack Mansell (former manager).

An atmospheric shot of players' kit laid out in the dressing room before a home game. The dressing rooms, home to many hundreds of Reading players over the last 102 seasons, will be demolished in June 1998, though supporters may have the opportunity to acquire items of furniture as souvenirs.

The Reading team and officials who lined up for the start of the 1997–98 season, the last at Elm Park. From left to right, back row: Ron Grant (kitman), Steve Swales, Andy Bernal, Phil Parkinson, Michael Thorp, Barry Hunter, Paul Holsgrove, Trevor Morley, Dariusz Wdowczyk, Alan Pardew (reserve-team coach); middle row: Paul Turner (physio), Keith McPherson, Paul Bodin, Sal Bibbo, Steve Mautone, Nicky Hammond, Stuart Lovell, Michael Meaker, Darren Caskey, Kevin Dillon (youth development); front row: Allan Harris (assistant manager), Ray Houghton, Martyn Booty, Byron Glasgow, Ben Smith, John Madejski (chairman), Terry Bullivant (manager), Nigel Howe (chief executive), Neville Roach, Andy Freeman, James Lambert, Martin Williams, Steve Kean (youth-team manager).

An aerial view of Elm Park during the final season of its existence. The club had made significant progress during the preceding ten years, and clearly needed to relocate to a larger, purpose-built stadium if that progress were to be continued.

Due to the relocation of Reading F.C. and on the joint instruction of

Reading Football Club plc

&

Salmon Harvester Properties Ltd

ELM PARK
FOOTBALL STADIUM
READING BERKSHIRE

6.30 acres (or 2.55 hectares) or thereabouts

RESIDENTIAL DEVELOPMENT SITE

TWO FREEHOLD LOTS FOR SALE
BY INFORMAL TENDER

With Vacant Possession Available Between
1st June 1998 to 1st October 1998

HASLAMS
Chartered Surveyors
SOLE AGENT

These particulars are intended only as a guide and must not be relied upon as a statement of fact.
Your attention is drawn to the important notice on the back cover of this brochure.

The front cover of the prospectus advertising the sale of Elm Park. Reading Borough Council had granted planning permission for the site to be developed for residential use allowing the erection of 128 housing units. The sale was due to be completed by 1 October 1998.

Chairman John Madejski is about to begin digging operations at the site of the new stadium, near junction 11 of the M4. The place where he is standing will be the centre-spot of the new pitch.

A model of the Madejski Stadium and Royal Berkshire Conference Centre as it will look when it opens in 1998. The new stadium has been designed with community and business partnership in mind, and will have an all-seated capacity of 25,000. Reading Football Club's opening match will be played there in August 1998, and will be an important landmark in the history of one of the oldest and most respected football clubs in the country.

Roll of Honour

The following people have expressed their continued support for Reading Football Club by including their names in this Roll of Honour:

Horace Cyril **Allen**
Henry James **Anderson**
John L. **Appleton**
Matthew Ryan **Atkins**
Michael **Ball**
David **Barley**
David **Barr**
Peter **Baxter**
Gerry **Bedding**
Val **Beltran**
Ian **Bilsby**
David James **Bird**
Colin **Blumenthal**
Andrew **Bonney**
David **Bowden**
Norman Eric **Bowden**
Kevin **Bradshaw**
Graham **Broadhurst**
Jeff **Broadhurst**
Oliver **Broadhurst**
Clive **Broster**
Robert **Burgess**
Susan **Campbell**
Peter **Capel**
Gareth **Carter**
Mark **Carter**
David **Clark**
Michael Stuart **Cliburn**
Simon **Coleby**

Michael **Collings**
David John **Collis**
Andrew Charles **Cove**
Mark 'Clunsey' **Cox**
Ian 'Duracell' **Crabb**
Brian John **Cradock**
John Robert **Croysdill**
Ray **Curry**
Geoffrey **Cutbush**
Michael John Christopher **Dare**
Christopher Patrick **Dawson**
Patrick Maurice **Dawson**
Gary Robert **Deards**
Nick **Deaves**
Gareth Charles **Dillaway**
David **Doe**
Trevor Charles **Douch**
Eddie **Dove**
Martin **Dove**
Peter **Dove**
Oliver **Dyer**
Edwin John **East**
John **Edmonds**
David **Edmunds**
Simon **Eedle**
Albert Walter **Englefield**
Keith Graham **Englefield**
Graham **Ford**

John **Freeman**
Christine Anne **French**
Julia M.E. **Gibson**
Michael **Gill**
James **Girdler**
Justin **Girdler**
Barbara Anne **Greenaway**
Barry **Greenaway**
Malcolm **Grismanauskas**
Alan **Hankin**
Rye **Harding**
Darren **Hawthorn**
Rachel **Hawthorn**
Simon **Hawthorn**
John Michael **Hayes**
Frank **Heywood**
Sandra **Heywood**
Paul Stephen **Hobbs**
Andrew James **Hood**
Darren **Jacobs**
Barry **Jones**
Roy **Jones**
Cyril **King**
Alison **Kingston**
Christopher **Kitley**
Joanna **Kitley**
Peter **Kitley**
Sarah **Kitley**
Cynthia **Lambert**

Joe **Leary**
Malcolm **Leary**
Jonathan Joseph **Lee**
Malcolm **Lee**
Stephen **Lewis**
John **Liddiard**
Andrew **Livsey**
Peter **Ludlow**
Matthew **Maitland**
Nigel **Maltby**
David John **Marney**
Christopher James Robert **Marshall**
Joshua Anthony **Marshall**
Kate Angela **Marshall**
Kevin Anthony **Marshall**
Pauline Angela **Marshall**
John **Martel**
Ron **McCulloch**
Charles Roy **Miles**
Trevor **Miles**
Robin Albert **Mills**
Howard **Morgan**
Jeff **Morgan**
Karen **Morgan**
Kevin **Morgan**
Robert **Morgan**
William **Morgan**
Christopher **Mulhern**
Paul **Munday**
Anne 'Nobby' **Newbery**
Kevin **Norris**
Stuart **Norris**
Jack **Overson**
Martin **Overson**
Dave **Peart**
Jamie Brian **Pettiford**
David **Pierce**
Matt **Pitman**
Steve **Pitman**
Cecily Laura **Platten**
Francis David John **Prior**
Adrian W. **Pye**
Brenda V.Y. **Pye**
David Charles **Quint**
Claire **Randall**
Derek **Randall**
Daniel Paul **Reid**
John James **Reid**
Spencer Joseph **Reid**
Peter **Rich**
David James **Richardson**

Christopher **Rose**
Ian **Rudd**
Stephen **Rudd**
David **Rush**
Mark Lee **Savin**
Ian Leslie **Scuffle**
Mike **Sharpe**
Peter John **Sharpe**
Tim **Shepherd**
Ann **Sherwood**
Julie Ann **Sherwood**
Nicholas **Sherwood**
Mark **Shrimpton**
Leonard John **Simms**
Arthur V. **Slater**
Andrew J. **Smallwood**
Jeremy **Smart**
Paul J.G. **Smith**
Peter J. **Smith**
Philip John **Smith**
Sandra M. **Smith**
Steve **Smith**
Alexander James **Stabler**
James Andrew **Stabler**
Luke Alexander **Stabler**
Jonathan **Stannett**
George Richard **Stephens**
Richard Hezlett **Stephens**
Kevin John **Stevens**
Bill **Stobie**
Brian **Stone**
Emma **Stone**
James **Stone**
Bill **Summers**
Adam **Sweetman**
Sarah **Sweetman**
Anton Fraser **Szklarek**
Helena M. **Szklarek**
Kathryn A. **Szklarek**
Dean Kevin **Thatcher**
Allen **Thompson**
Claire **Thrussell**
Simon **Thrussell**
Roger **Titford**
Laurence Christopher **Toft**
Steven **Topazio**
David Paul **Townsend**
Michael James **Townsend**
Paul **Townsend**
Chris **Tubb**
Leslie **Tubb**
Michael **Tubb**

Peter **Tubb**
Phillip Roy **Tubb**
Roy Barrie **Tubb**
William **Tubb**
Edward **Upton**
Elizabeth Peta **Upton**
Tracey Elizabeth **Upton**
Marc **Van de Velde**
David **Wallbank**
Philip 'Milkshake' **Warner**
Robert Alan **Webb**
Chris P. **Wilkins**
Shirley M. **Wilkins**
Stuart M.R. **Wilkinson**
Andrew John **Wilson**
Donald W.A. **Wilson**
Ray **Winter**
Reg **Winter**
Arthur Charles **Withers**
Alex **Wood**
Evangeline **Wood**
Barry Glyn **Woodyer**
Dennis John **Woodyer**
Ronald Cecil James **Woodyer**